Numerological Horoscope
The millennial method to understand what awaits us in the coming year

VITIANA PAOLA MONTANA

Copyright © 2017 Vitiana Paola Montana

All right reserved

ISBN:1974634515
ISBN-13:9781974634514

DEDICATION

I dedicate this small book, a useful reminder to be used in the study, to all those willing students who have shown me so much affection and commitment in the learning of Evolutionary Numerology.

TABLE OF CONTENTS

	Acknowledgments	i
1	About Me	1
2	INTRODUCTION	4
3	ESOTERIC AND SYMBOLIC MEANING OF NUMBERS – THE MEANING OF NUMBER 1 IN NUMEROLOGY	10
4	THE MEANING OF NUMBER 2 IN NUMEROLOGY	14
5	THE MEANING OF NUMBER 3 IN NUMEROLOGY	18
6	THE MEANING OF NUMBER 4 IN NUMEROLOGY	22
7	THE MEANING OF NUMBER 5 IN NUMEROLOGY	27
8	THE MEANING OF NUMBER 6 IN NUMEROLOGY	31
9	THE MEANING OF NUMBER 7 IN NUMEROLOGY	34
10	THE MEANING OF NUMBER 8 IN NUMEROLOGY	38
11	THE MEANING OF NUMBER 9 IN NUMEROLOGY	41

12	HOW TO CALCULATE YOUR PERSONAL NUMBERS	11
13	HOW TO BUILD A NUMEROLOGY CHART	47
14	WHAT'S A PERSONAL YEAR	49
15	HOW TO CALCULATE THE PERSONAL YEAR	52
16	PERSONAL YEAR 1	56
17	PERSONAL YEAR 2	62
18	PERSONAL YEAR 3	65
19	PERSONAL YEAR 4	68
20	PERSONAL YEAR 5	71
21	PERSONAL YEAR 6	74
22	PERSONAL YEAR 7	77
23	PERSONAL YEAR 8	80
24	PERSONAL YEAR 9	83
25	HOW TO USE NUMEROLOGY	86
26	FINAL THOUGHT	92

ACKNOWLEDGMENTS

My thinking goes to the great Masters who devoted their lives to the study of those disciplines designed to create greater awareness in humans. I therefore thank all those who have embarked on the journey before me and from whom I have learned everything. I formed through study, reflection and exercise. The only ways to go their own way.

1
ABOUT ME

My name is Vitiana Paola Montana and I'm a researcher and expert of symbols, numerology and Kabbalah since over 30 years.

Symbols have been a constant presence during my whole life, and carefully analyzing their precious meanings I've enforced my intuition and the knowledge of exoteric disciplines.

First among these disciplines is for me the Jewish Kabbalah, also known as "Door to Knowledge" as it requires you to cultivate your spiritual evolution for a true inner growth.

While exploring Numerology I've been studying and analyzing archetypes and the Major Arcana Tarots iconography.

Bringing together the characteristics of both disciplines I've delivered lectures and courses to teach my method: an approach to understanding that takes into account every human facet: physical, psychic, emotional, evolutional and spiritual.

This is the method I'm using in creating my "Numerology Charts" for those who request them through my website.

My personal blog is Progetto Evolutivo, where I write (in Italian) about these and other related subjects, besides the Numerologica website which is more strictly related to the topics discussed in this book.

Enjoy the reading!

2
INTRODUCTION

Numerology and Personal Year.

Among old sayings the "New Year New Life" proverb has certainly a place of honor. Considering the problems and challenges we're all facing nowadays, it's more than a wish. In this ebook you're going to learn how to decode your personal year and get the best from the arising data.

In the following pages I'm going to explain how you can discover your "personal year" and, following my directions, analyze the main aspects, challenges and opportunities that await you in the new year.

Of course this analysis is going to produce a different result for each person, as it's based on the birth date. Everything will be clearly explained in the forthcoming chapters, and it's easier done than said, so don't worry.

Before anything else, by the way, I want to plead Numerology's cause, as this discipline has been too often trivialized or depicted as a sort of entertaining activity.

In fact, it's very easy to find online tools which offer numerology answers generated by automatic software calculations.

A Numerology Chart created by a Numerologist can reach, because of its richness of information and numerous numerology facets examined, a length of 80/90, and even 100 pages.

As you can see, Numerologists' analysis

reports have nothing in common with those automatic tools you find online or in certain software programs.

Numerology is an esoteric discipline with thousands years in its history, it's a window open on the Universe and cannot be wrapped up in a computer program. Pythagoras used to say that "everything is number", thus numbers are symbols of reality.

The same concept is expressed in Jewish Kabbalah: according to this discipline the Sephirots (paths), substances emanated from the Divine Light of the Creator, can be referred to numbers. To better explain this concept, we could say that "number is the archetype of symbol".

Understanding the meaning of numbers in Numerology, thus, allows you to decipher Nature's secrets, guiding your intuition towards the real meaning and message contained in each number.

Don't worry if everything still looks obscure and prolix, you'll soon be able to decipher your personal numerological patterns thanks to the instructions given in the following pages.

You'll see how exciting it is to calculate your personal year number and explore its meaning as I'll explain the esoteric and symbolic meaning of numbers from 1 to 9 in the following pages, but there's still an important point to note: Pythagoras, cabbalists and medieval alchemists have always considered numbers as individual symbols of a secret code.

Every human event, thus, has a numerological significance in its manifestation, and because of this there's a numerological interpretation of it.

You may ask: is it possible, then, to

forecast events, situations and circumstances?

Not exactly. Each one of us has the power of "free will" and is thus able to exercise his/her "right to choose" in (almost) every situation.

We can't talk about "numerological soothsaying" or "precognition" without risking to drift into the not so noble realm of those who take advantage of such a noble art as Numerology just as a commercial tool to make money.

Diligently and consciously studying your own personal numbers is an exercise of thought and meditation. It means turning inside ourselves and seek for our deepest essence.

Numerology, as I use it in this guide, is a way to take readers by hand and guide them, in small steps, in really knowing themselves and their personality and life, observing themselves from the inside with the help of their own personal numbers.

And now get ready to discover what's in store for you during the new coming year. Get ready with paper and pencil, the adventure begins!

Have a Good Reading and a Good Life!

3
ESOTERIC AND SYMBOLIC MEANING OF NUMBERS

The Meaning of Number 1 in Numerology

Let's start this fascinating path of discovery, about the meaning of the numbers. Number 1 is the only principle, the origin of all things. According to Jewish Kabbalah, who studies the mysteries of the Torah (the Jewish Bible), there are numerous correspondences between numbers, letters, and reality.

Through the insights of Gematria (the 'decoding' tool of the Torah), we can discover many different levels of meaning for our numbers.

Each of the 22 letters of the Hebrew alphabet has a numeric value, a corresponding sound, and a specific type of energy. Number 1 is associated with the letter Aleph (א). In this case, it represents Man, the first creature born of God; it represents the Will, the Perfect Action.

We see, then, that the essential aspect of the One, after the zero, about which we will talk on another occasion, is the underlying unit of all Creation. It is the first "Number One", that belongs to that category of digits that are divisible only for themselves.

The One is the bearer of new cycles, of new ideas, is the courage and the mastery that join to manifest themselves in the actions we accomplish.

Pythagoras claimed that numbers from 1 to 9, divided into groups, are symbols of different energies:

9 and 8 form Emotional Energy
7, 6 and 5 form Intuitive Energy
4, 3, 2 and 1 form Mental Energy

And here's the 1 in the group that represents Mental Energy. This means that it is the Thought that creates our reality. You certainly have heard about the "Law of Attraction".

So, the One encloses the root of thought and action that, joined, create reality. To understand more deeply the true meaning of numbers, we will also explore their esoteric meaning.

If we search in the dictionary the term "esoteric", we will find that it comes from the

Greek ESÔTERIKÔS whose root is ESÔTERÔS, meaning "interior".

So, the name Esoteric was adopted for Pythagoras' disciples invited into the school, where they could see the philosopher and attend his lessons; as opposed to the "outsiders" who were called EXOTÈRICS by the Greek EXTERIOR.

Number One, by its creative features, has always been associated with the Sun in astrological sense. We will see how such correspondences are also present for the other digits.

The Journey into the World of Numbers has just begun.

4
THE MEANING OF NUMBER 2 IN NUMEROLOGY

In numerology, number 2 is called the "Great Mother" or "Nurturer". The Two has female characteristic as it is associated with the creation, the birth, the descent of the breath of the Spirit in matter.

It is also part of the group of numbers that form Mental Energy. Being the expression of "gestation," this number attests the conception of the embryo, whether it is a birth, an idea, a deliberate act, or an evolutionary process. Number 2 is also associated with "lunar dualism", the two expressions of the female side Isis and Hecate, "the goddess with black face."

Isis, the luminous moon power, the power of nature, the cycles, the tides, the water of life. And then Hecate, the dark side, the strength of the Earth's bowels. In the past, this particular definition was seen in a negative light.

The dark side of Hecate, in the feminine, is certainly not synonymous with negative or bad. These are exclusive intuitive qualities of the female unconscious in particular, which have always aroused fears because of their power implications and have created feelings of control by society and, above all, in religious institutions.

Let us not forget the witch hunt in the dark Middle Ages when every talent in a woman was seen as devil's work!

In fact, intuitive power, mental power, telluric energies of the menstrual cycle are powerful channels that empower the communication of woman with herself and with the forces of nature, whose laws she welcomes and manifests more than any other living being.

The Two, therefore, expresses receptivity, harmony, great sensitivity and imagination. In Kabbalah, the Two is associated with the second letter of the Hebrew alphabet: Beit (ב). Its esoteric meaning is "mouth" (in the sense of nourishment-nurturing) and "home" (hearth, family).

From this details one understands how number 2 is considered the expression of Woman as Mother, as it corresponds to the quality of cooperation and equilibrium.

The Power of Female Energy nourishes, cares, protects and sustains; at the same time it grows and increases itself while giving.

5
THE MEANING OF NUMBER 3 IN NUMEROLOGY

Considered the "perfect number" as the expression of the Triad or Trinity, Number Three is associated with Jupiter, representing authority, the sense of duty brought to its highest expression.

It is the spiritual symbol of the plant that extends its branches (trifurcation) and the Pythagoreans considered it sacred because it allows tracing the triangle, perfect figure.

If we recall the Greek mythology we studied at school, we will remember to have heard several times about these divinities: the Params, the Furies, the Thanks, always in number three.

The Three is the result of the union between One, the active principle and the Two, the womb that embraces creation. We can call it the first product of thought that multiplies and expands; It encloses both the concept of union and the expansion.

The Three is the Son of the Father (1) and of the Mother (2), who formed through the Breath of Life and can thus continue the Species.

In the profound meaning of the term "Trinity," we find many references to "perfection". This term must not be interpreted literally. In fact, it goes far beyond any aesthetic, external meaning, which it might recall. We have, however, to associate it with the superior qualities of the One, the Two and the Three.

Perfection is the harmony of the parts; it is the balance of the forces. Perfection is "to create" anything (thoughts, actions, material expressions) with the strength and righteousness of the One, with the grace and fertility of the Two and keep all this in perfect harmony to make it grow and expand.

According to Kabbalah, the Three is associated with the third letter of the Hebrew alphabet: Ghimel (ג). The letter's shape recalls that of someone in the act of running, as putting his foot forward to gain momentum.

This is the origin of the movement, it is the push to exit from oneself, from the limitations that duality proposes us continually (wrong/right, good/bad, positive/negative).

Ghimel, the Three, is the seat of the willingness to grow, it's what invites us to activity, to progress, to the improvement of what we are.

We need to get out of our habits, from what limits us and directs us towards the true self, towards the most true, deep and eternal part of ourselves.

The form of Ghimel also represents the expansion and contraction of Infinite Light during the process of creating the Worlds.

Remember the contractions and the release in the labor of childbirth.

It is no coincidence that in order to be born again to ourselves, we must first gather, reflect and then expand our consciousness in a new way, creating our new life.

6
THE MEANING OF NUMBER 4 IN NUMEROLOGY

Four is the number of foundations, of stability, of basics, of "system". It is the first square number (2^2).

Associated with the Earth, it is present in the "quaternary groupings": the seasons, the angles, the elements, the cardinal points. It also represents the four doors the neophyte has to go through before entering the Temple of Life.

These four doors are connected to the four

elements: **Fire**, **Earth**, **Air**, **Water**.

This is the path of discovery that man walks to "go home", that is, to re-gain himself and his divine power. By experimenting with the characteristics of each element, the human being progresses, regains its fullness, recognizes its charisma and evolves.

Fire sends strength, courage, and passion for what is important to achieve in our lives.

Earth allows us to dwell on the seeds of our intellect, to plant new expressions of ourselves in order to germinate them safe from the storms of life, to grow them and let them bear their fruits.

Air corresponds to the vivid intelligence that is expressed in freedom, drawing on the millennial knowledge of symbols and archetypes, giving us the breath that leads to "understanding."

Water, the Source of Life or "Water of the Spirit", is the nourishment without which the seed can't grow: it is unconditional love through which "everything flourishes".

The exact sequence of the elements is reported in the Progress of the Zodiacal Signs. Let's look at it:

- Aries - Cardinal Sign (Fire)

- Taurus - Fixed Sign (Earth)

- Gemini - Mutable Sign (Air)

- Cancer - Cardinal Sign (Water)

- Lion - Fixed Sign (Fire)

- Virgin - Mutable Sign (Earth)

- Libra - Cardinal Sign (Air)

- Scorpio - Fixed Sign (Water)

- Sagittarius - Mutable Sign (Fire)

- Capricorn - Cardinal Sign (Earth)

- Aquarium - Fixed Sign (Air)

- Fish - Mutable Sign (Water)

Observe the list carefully and note the regular cadence of the items.

It takes exactly three complete four-step sequences to complete the Zodiac cycle. These three cycles reflect the sequence of human life stages: from birth to 27 years, from 28 years to 55 and from 56 years ahead. There are challenges, changes and experiences in each cycle. Humanistic Numerology and Kabbalah help us deepen the understating of these steps and use them constructively in our evolutionary process.

In Kabbalah, Four is associated with the fourth letter of the Hebrew alphabet: Daleth (ד). Daleth means "door", yet another correspondence, therefore, to the importance of looking for our true self with absolute simplicity, safe from the ego's influences.

Recognizing our own divine nature without being overwhelmed by egocentrism, teaches us how to be masters of ourselves.

7
THE MEANING OF NUMBER 5 IN NUMEROLOGY

The general meaning of Number Five is associated with experimenting, the actual knowledge of facts, the evolving process, the "status change" in a situation.

Corresponds to Hermes in Greek mythology. It is the Psychopomp that guides the souls of the departed to the kingdom of the dead.

Its symbols are Kerukeion, or Caduceus, a wand with snakes wrapped around the stem, and winged sandals. His counterpart in Roman mythology is Mercury, messenger of gods.

Hence, its particular facilitator role in moving from an emotional, mental and physical state to a new condition. Like in mythology, he accompanies our "state passages", acting on emotional conditions.

Symbol of dynamism, intelligence and curiosity brings with it the tendency to approach, sometimes even dangerously, boundaries and transgressions.

Number Five is linked to the fifth letter of the Hebrew alphabet: Hey (ה), which means intuition, illumination.

The Kabbalists identify three stages for the Hey letter, which lay down on three different levels, subsequent to the development of awareness.

The first, the lowest, is Hey and corresponds to a scream of fear (Ohi!), The first lament of the newly born child.

It is the pain of the Soul, which is a part of infinity which, when it is born, realizes that it has taken the limits of the body and is dependent on physical needs.

Continuing, we have the second level, the intermediate one, where Hey becomes the expression of a nice surprise (Oh!). This is the feeling of joy for their free and independent life, which is experienced when individual talents are realized.

The pain of birth is overcome by happiness and enthusiasm in discovering how much harmony and fertility is present in the world. Finally, we have the highest level in the word Hine = Here! We come here to understand the divine presence within our existence.

So Hey becomes, on this level, the letter of

inner rebirth.

Number Five is the number of self-expression force. Specifically, it refers to the skill of speaking (see Mercury, skilled beguiler).

And in fact, the physical components corresponding to the ability in speaking are exactly five: tongue, teeth, palate, lips, throat.

Precisely because of the complex interaction between intellect and word, the number Five suggests that we use any kind of inner discipline in order to "ferry" our personality, from a state of unease/dissatisfaction to the desired state.

Only by ruling the communication, the expression of ideas, feelings and facts, we can reach a balanced exchange and grow.

8
THE MEANING OF NUMBER 6 IN NUMEROLOGY

Number 6 describes Harmony and deep commitment in any kind of relationships. It represents the encounter of man with his ultimate choice: the divine or the corruption of matter.

The Pythagoreans expressed this number using the hexagram indicating the adept, or "the one who has not yet chosen".

Associated with Venus and Isthar, it had an important role in ancient mysteries because it represented the six dimensions of all bodies.

It is considered one of the perfect numbers being the result of both the multiplication and the addiction of the triad:

1 x 2 x 3 = 6   1 + 2 + 3 = 6

Number Six suggests the need, from a psychological point of view, of learning how to integrate one's ideals and values with reality.

Only in this way, in fact, our existence can be defined "balanced" and capable of producing a constant evolution.

According to Kabbalah, Six is equivalent to the sixth letter of the Hebrew alphabet: the Vav (ו) meaning extension, connection.

This letter also means "hook" suggesting the importance of connecting with others. The Vav represents our ability to establish lasting and high-level relationships with each other by "engaging" us to create collaborative ideas, businesses and useful and constructive projects.

9
THE MEANING OF NUMBER 7 IN NUMEROLOGY

Often related to spirituality, number 7 has, in fact, many other features such as intuition, the ability to blend magic and reality, the ability to "realize" magic in everyday life.

For Pythagoreans, it was the number of cyclic perfection, geometrically associated with the circle.

Expression of Neptune, god of the sea, has many correspondences in his work: the seven sins, the seven seas, the musical notes, the days of the week, the seven angels of the Revelation, the Pleiades and the seven constellations.

When this number appears in a numerological report, eventually in several places, it states that the individual who holds it possesses remarkable spiritual, charismatic gifts.

When more Seven appear in a numerology report, we can say with reasonable certainty that we are in the presence of an individual gifted with important talents, some of which still to be expressed.

There is a small similarity that has been used by the wise men, since ancient times, which clearly conveys the idea of Seven's nature.

Imagine a dark cavern where you can see floating in the darkness a beautiful flower that sheds light by virtue of its inner wisdom and beauty.

A beautiful bright flower.

This flower remains hidden, because it doesn't esteem its own beauty; he's afraid of truly showing itself in the light since it thinks that may cause pain and rejection.

Often, the Seven have this wrong image of themselves (and, sometimes, not just them).

That's why, in such a case, we will have to look through the numerology report and find the individual's turning points to offer a better guidance and offer the right support in integrating all aspects of personality. According to Kabbalah, Seven is associated with the letter Zain (ז).

This letter means "instrument of war" and refers to the conflict within the nature of man.

The instrument we are talking about is necessary in spiritual life and is used to remove all that prevents us from continuing our growth.

10
THE MEANING OF NUMBER 8 IN NUMEROLOGY

The meaning of number 8 is linked to the symbol of Infinity, victory, karma, and money as energy.

Number 8 represents fertility and prosperity. Esoterically, it is connected to the blindfolded Justice that holds the two scales, the intellect that rises above what is earthly.

We find it in sacred architecture, with octagonal shape. Astrologically linked to Saturn, this number embodies the symbol of perfection, the perpetual course of the universe.

Those with an Eight in their birth date can expect a challenging task: they are here to transcend abundance and power, placing them at the service of a higher cause, rather than pursuing them as an end to themselves.

Until they have found their balance and haven't learnt to express their power, they will always be victims of their emotional extremes.

In this path, the spiritual side of existence will be very important; to develop this aspect of one's personality they will be forced to conform to the mystical side of life. In Kabbalah, the Eight corresponds to the letter Cheit (ח).

Cheit is called the "double door". It is the door through which the unborn comes into light, but it is also the gateway to the spiritual revival of man.

In Kabbalah, the Eight is the entry into the dimension beyond time, and in this case it's seen horizontally and becomes the symbol of the Infinite, the Greek Lemniscate ∞.

.

11
THE MEANING OF NUMBER 9 IN NUMEROLOGY

In Greece, this number was given special consideration.

Defined as Ennea, it was identified with the nine-pointed star, built with three equilateral triangles tied together.

The same Greek mythology brings the Nine in connection with the Nine Muses of which Terpsichore, the muse of sacred dance, is the ninth and the most powerful.

Symbol of Moon and Hecate, Nine is linked to the descent of energy into matter.

In addition to representing the full cycle of transmutation, it is the expression of judgment at the moment of death.

Astrologically it corresponds to Mars, a lord of war and strength, and is therefore defined as totally yang. A subject with number Nine in birth denotes passion, impulsiveness and will.

Nine's connotations are, from the moral point of view, integrity and wisdom. These are the values that an evolved Nine casts to the outside world: these individuals drive and inspire with their example.

Nine's Life Purpose requires them to live up to the high standard of existence. Being deep and charismatic, they often find themselves in roles of leadership.

Their challenge is in fact to reach wisdom getting through, recognizing and elaborating their own emotions.

Kabbalistically, Nine is associated with the letter Tet (ט). Tet means "command stick" and the evidence that is being submitted is to learn how to handle that part of our personality that aspires to power and command.

Especially because of this feature, the Nine is also called the "Number of Truth."

.

12
HOW TO CALCULATE YOUR PERSONAL NUMBERS

Each one of us has 7 specific numbers that, together, create a complete definition of ourselves. Let's see what these numbers are:

- **Expression Number** (given by the sum of the value of each letter in our name and surname); this number describes our character, our skills, our love and friendship, our work and our health.

- **Motivation Number** (given by the sum of the value of each vowel in our name and surname); this number underlines our deep and unrevealed ambitions. It shows the kind of individual we want to be, even if it's different from the way we appear right now, and reveals what we look for in life. This number also tells if we're in balance with ourselves.

- **Realization Number** (given by the sum of the value of consonants in our name and surname); it reveals the way we're going to realize ourselves in life, but also what's the first impact we have on others.
- **Active Name** (it's the complete sum of the values of letters in our birth name); this number influences the Expression Number. It's an evidence of our qualities or a reduce the negative tendencies of character.
- **Hereditary Number** (it's the sum of the value of all letters in the family name); this is another number influencing the Expression

Number, albeit more lightly.

- **Destiny Number** (it's the sum of all numbers in the our birth date); this is a fundamental number! It shows us the path we're going to follow in our life, including the challenges, the obstacles or easy paths we're going to find along the road.

- **Balancer** (it's the value we obtain summing the Expression Number and the Destiny Number); this numbers talks about our character and our personality, and underlines the role they have in our professional life.

The energetic value projected by this number have a great influence in our life, mostly after the age of 29.

.

13
HOW TO BUILD A NUMEROLOGY CHART

In order to build a Numerology Chart you need to include in the process both the numbers from 1 to 9 and the Master Numbers (11, 22, 33).

Each letter of our full name (birth name, included additional names, and family name) must be converted to a number using the following table to calculate their values:

1 = A J S

2 = B K T

3 = C L U

4 = D M V

5 = E N W

6 = F O X

7 = G P Y

8 = H Q Z

9 = I

14
WHAT'S A PERSONAL YEAR

Many of us, probably more than once, have felt the need to focus on the closing year, trying to evaluate the months just passed away in a perspective of results and challenges for the coming year.

Everything flows in our mind while a cycle of our life is closing and a new one is facing us with all the dreams and wishes we'll try to make true.

What has the new year in store for us? Will I succeed in having a new home, a new relationship, a new job? Is this the right year for having a baby? Questions like these arise in our mind often long before the last day of December leaves the place to the first day of a new year.

Yet, inside ourselves we already have a trace of what we would like to realize in the forthcoming new cycle.

To face important decisions the right way or best evaluate the chances or the outcome of an event we must always make better use of our rationality and common sense.

But if we want to have a wider view of the circumstances we're going to analyze, we must allow our subconscious to interact with that part of our mind we use in daily life.

The logical, practical side of our personality absolutely needs the support of our intuition, the "sixth sense" offered by our subconscious mind that offers an optimal, global view of things.

How to obtain this global view? How to master the rational and intuitive sides of our mind making them work together towards the building of a wider and more complete vision?

Besides an open attitude towards everything that appears as "new" and "different" from our ordinary way of viewing things, we can use our "Personal Year".

Let's see what it is in detail, then, and how to obtain.

15
HOW TO CALCULATE THE PERSONAL YEAR

Numerology teaches us that every solar year is connected to a specific number and is an expression of its qualities. There are two kind of annuity:

Universal Year and Personal Year. To calculate the first you simply sum up that year digits, for example our 2014 will be a Universal Year "number 7".

A 7 Year will have specific aspects politically, economically and socially and its influence will be visible in daily life if we learn to recognize every important event that occurs.

Globally, in a Universal Year 7 there's going to be some sort of "pause", a period of reflections both by governments and individuals about the best choices towards a better living and the search for a solution, at least a structural one, to the most urgent problems they're facing.

I'm going to analyze the Universal Year concept in a forthcoming ebook, while studying the Personal Year in these pages.

It's easy to calculate your Personal Year: just sum up your day and month of birth together with the forthcoming year digits.

Here's an example:

John is born on September 15, 1978.

To know his personal year 2017 we'll make this simple calculation:

15 (day of birth) + 9 (September, month of birth) + 2 + 0 + 1 + 7 = 25 = 7

For John the year 2017 is a 7 Year.

We must also take care to remember the two digits value from which we derive the final number, in this case 25.

The meaning of this number is very important, in particular if it's one of the Master Numbers (11, 22, 33).

Summing these two digits we obtain the final, single digit of the year number, and this latter will be analyzed both individually and eventually in its relationship with a Master Number if this is present.

In the following pages you'll find details about the meaning of each Personal Year so you'll be able to learn and recognize their influence on your daily life.

16
PERSONAL YEAR 1

Before describing the Personal Year 1 it's very important to discuss the concept of personal year in a wider perspective.

Every individual, in fact, goes through a complete yearly cycle. According to our birth date, when we decide to find at which point of the cycle we are now (for example if we are in year 4 or 5) it's very important to focus on a "global view" of that cycle. Let me explain it better in the following lines.

Every evolutional path, both from a

personal and from a psychological and professional point of view, requires an awareness of the "message" that each year brings to us.

Thus, wherever we are in our path right now, the first thing to do is to clarify our starting point. In order to correctly follow our path we need, then, to become aware of our present reality and look at it objectively, thus understanding its influence on our personal life.

So, let's go on with the analysis of a Year 1, I'm sure you'll understand more easily what I've just expressed above.

The personal year tells us exactly what we should put into practice during its flow. These are actions, choices, changes or consolidations that are going to enrich our growth path.

Within a personal year, there is a sub-cycle consisting of the months which regulates, most incisively, all the flow of the year in question.

This topic will be discussed in a forthcoming ebook, often visiting www.numerologica.it because other initiatives will soon be presented.

A Personal Year cycle obviously begins with a Year 1, which represents the time when the foundations for new projects, for new ideas are laid; Is a stage of rebirth.

We can consider Year 1 as the ideal time to start something new, to be determined to change an aspect of our lives that no longer responds to the new needs that are outlining.

Year 1 drives you to change direction in the things you are doing, invites you to have the courage to try to realize your dreams.

Being essentially a propulsion of change, year 1 relates to everything that leads to renewal, exploring new opportunities, using new attitudes to change its approach to life. It is an invitation to trust, to be determined to believe in their own possibilities.

If you are preparing for a Year 1, reflect on what you want, about what's in your heart. Choose what you want to create, with all the honesty and objectivity you are capable of, deciding what is to be born in this new year.

Look for what you are deeply entertained, what makes you happy and dedicated to developing this trend.

It may be a personal transformation (such as modifying or containing a defect, or a value to exalt), or a retraining of your professional skills.

In any case, the advice of year 1 is to make a careful check of our personal situation and to act accordingly, drawing up a project of accomplishment that gives us enthusiasm, strength and especially the purpose to concretize it.

So begin by listing the things you want to achieve or accomplish. There may also be small improvements in daily life, such as changing dietary habits or incorporating exercise into your daily activities.

It is, therefore, to "start" something new, to plan and implement it, helping with the most consistant, determined and most important ingredient: enthusiasm.

Keywords for Year 1: Renewal, Exploration, Responsibility.

17
PERSONAL YEAR 2

We just started the new nine-year cycle. The year 1, recently explored, has begun to concretize the new projects, the desired changes.

With year 2, we get into a "stasis" observation dimension after the start of new activities. We enter, that is, in a phase of slow development of the initiatives we have given course.

After all the planning of last year, we now need to work on the details of the projects /

ideas / challenges / changes we have decided to undertake. One year 2 may seem like a slowdown, in fact it is a step of integration between the chosen target and its actualization.

You may encounter obstacles or people who limit your path, so it's important not to be overwhelmed by anxiety and not adopt unsuitable attitudes to developing ongoing projects.

Be assured that all this is more than natural and do not worry if you find nothing significant is happening for your initiatives.

This is just the natural settling, among other things, necessary for everything that is growing.

Commit to developing diplomacy, touch and cultivating friendships. Be available to others in the right measure, without allowing selfishness and too much possessiveness to others, distract you from your goals.

Very important will be your determination to maintain balance and constancy in continuing on the line you have undertaken.

Keywords for Year 2: Commitment, Balance, Constancy.

18
PERSONAL YEAR 3

Let's go now with the personal year 3. The energy span of Year 1 fused with the patience, constancy and balance of Year 2.

Proceed with projects, reflect on what to do, locate the Right strategies and proper resource management are the main activities of year 2.

Now, with Year 3, we need to "synthesize" the results of these first two years of the cycle.

It will be crucial to combine the 1's momentum with the reflective condensation of 2 and carry these two phases to a fusion that brings "action."

To do this, you will have to get rid of the sense of constraint you inevitably presented with year 2, you will have to be able to shake off the probable conditioning due to the need to keep control of the momentum and enthusiasm.

To do so, to give space to the creative part of Year 3, it may be useful to free the playful part that is in you. Try to put the rigor behind and free the imagination.

Get out of the shell by doing something new, learning a new hobby, changing power, wearing a dress of a color absent from your wardrobe, changing itinerary as you go to work.

They are all "actions" that help the creative part to emerge and put roots. The reason why you should make this choice is that, by doing so, your left side of the brain, stimulated by these initiatives, begins to produce new ideas, new solutions to the challenges and goals you have developed in the first two years of the cycle.

So take this year 3 to make your creative side flourish and consolidate, in Year 4 you will have to work very intensively.

Keywords for Year 3: Lightness, Creativity, Communicative.

19
PERSONAL YEAR 4

After experiencing the liberating force of the creativity of year 3, it is now time to reorder everything that has emerged in paths or initiatives.

In Personal Year 4, you will feel the need to calm down, reorganize your mind and energies.

Now is the time to reflect on your personal goals and plan a short-term plan to bring about something concrete and tangible.

Build for your future, take responsibility

and follow your projects very carefully.

This phase of further review may lead you to be more critical than usual; Could push you to affirm your point of view more forcefully and raise new challenges while attaining your goals. Now you are more determined and fighting.

Just because you are safer than you, your feelings, and your ideas, there may be changes even in the environment around you.

First, this new state will work on your close associates, from a professional point of view. Secondly, parental relationships will also have a good influence on your new position.

I emphasize the sequence of this state change. It will leave the working environment to extend to the family and not the opposite.

This is because your personal position will be re-evaluated and will grow first and foremost in the work environment.

This passage will bring with it a series of reflections and evaluations that will inevitably also have a positive effect on relationships with close family members.

Therefore, to be more assertive in the profession, for once, will have a good record in personal relationships.

Keywords for Year 4: Assertiveness, Reorganization, Building the Future

20
PERSONAL YEAR 5

The Year 5 is comparable to an injection of adrenaline. This is a year of change.

The actions you have taken up to this point have supported your personal path. You are at the heart of your nine-year cycle, so expect new and unexpected news, especially in the second half of the year.

So be receptive to everything that comes again. Take into account the chance to see real shots of luck.

Have the clarity of catching these

opportunities with the necessary caution. In this new breeding phase, there will be advantages and opportunities for new jobs.

In the perspective of proposing and getting in the game, do not be modest. Study well how to promote yourself and advertise your person and your projects.

Make a point of engagement in hiking and in increasing your social life. People, in this special time, are attracted to your energy and the enthusiasm you send.

Year 5 brings with it additional responsibilities. In addition to expanding your network of contacts, promoting your public image, you also have an eye on everything regarding any contracts you are going to make.

Make sure all agreements are respected, you will avoid problems and delays.

The suggestion to increase the results

achieved throughout this year is to maximize efforts in applying the display to the results you want to achieve.

Make a pact with yourself and dedicate all the attention you deserve, you will succeed in winning what you want.

Keywords for Year 5: energy, affirmation, display.

21
PERSONAL YEAR 6

Personal Year 6 is a good time to create a more harmonious atmosphere in your environment.

By year 5, you've learned to take on more responsibilities, you are committed to enhancing your interaction with other environments and expanding your reach.

You will now use these features to bring added value to each relationship / relationship you have in place, applying everything you learned to the context in which you live. The key to understanding this year is that you are learning to share and share everything you've received in abundance.

Whether you are attentive, resourceful, supportive or anything else, you can integrate it perfectly at the present moment. You have to avoid impulsive actions, leaving aside the ego and the wrong attitudes.

Ethics and morals will be the two qualities that will accompany you throughout your Year 6.

You may find yourself at the beginning of the year having difficulty in implementing this behavior. The first month of this year could be very challenging from an energetic and mental point of view.

Start every activity, every project, with a lot of calmness and rely on determination to pursue the goals you have set.

As the weeks run, there will be

improvements and you can return to have more clarity on everything.

I favored everything that brings renewal, especially in the summer months: holidays, new interests, renewing the home, starting a new hobby, learning a new language.

Keywords for Year 6: Apply Values, Renew, Communicate

22
PERSONAL YEAR 7

The Personal Year 7 is one of the most important in the cycle of the nine.

It is at its beginnings, in fact, that a general review is made of the years that preceded it. If you remember, at the end of the previous chapter, I have already reminded you of this important review by reflecting on your personal values and their application to everyday life.

One Year 7, you see yourself committed to reevaluating everything you've done so far. It is a break in the cycle that allows you to look back and analyze and integrate everything you have done in recent years.

The advice is to be detached and to try to understand what is no longer working in your life, what it slows down or keeps you tight, imprisoned.

To do this in the best way, to have clarity of intent and discover your most precious sides, stay "centered" in yourself, bring concentration to your everyday life and refine your introspection ability.

Inevitably, you will be slowed down by reflection. In any case, the recommendation is to undertake the path with the necessary calm and serenity necessary to complete the review.

Because of these checks, many of your relationships will be questioned, from sentimental relationships, to professional relationships.

You will, by using comparison and dialogue, eliminate misunderstandings and explain better what your primary needs are: people will understand.

Keywords for Year 7: Assertiveness, Detachment, Review.

23
PERSONAL YEAR 8

New energy and new lifeblood. An important, laborious, busy and busy year is waiting for you.

You will be called to choose more than once in the twelve months. Choices, decisions, will affect all areas of life.

In year 7 you had to complete a complete review of your lifestyle. There have been things that you have left running, reports that you closed because they looked like dried branches, work collaborations that followed the same fate or were re-evaluated and remounted on the road.

In this year, you will have to put each piece back in place. After a long time, finally rediscover your ambition and recognize the value of your personal power.

Now is the time to make fundamental decisions, after reflecting, elaborating and choosing for the whole of the previous period.

Year 8 represents success in the cycle of nine. Feel more security, you are comfortable in situations, you know who you are and where you are going.

Your assertiveness makes you authoritative even with yourself: you will test yourself and evaluate in a totally objective way, even the results you will get.

At the end of December you will be satisfied with everything you did this year, bringing with you the results of your spiritual development. Year 9 is at the door.

Keywords for Year 8: Success, Renewal, Personal Power.

24
PERSONAL YEAR 9

It's time to complete, harvest. A year 9 is the beginning of a new cycle, previewing on Year 1.

In these months, in fact, you have the first rumors of what the New Year is preparing for you. There will be the condensation of the changes you have triggered with the review of Years 7 and 8.

An important step for year 9 is the conclusion of everything you started. You must be able to start the Year 1, the first of a new cycle, completely free from any trajectory, from suspended things.

Everything that comes to life, from now on, has a new form, it is the result of your personal change and therefore needs to be born in a new environment.

Let go of the old man, detach yourself from people who somehow subtract energy and make room for new knowledge that, on the contrary, enrich you and support you.

Place orders in your home, in closets, drawers, in the garage. Get rid of everything you do not need anymore and make room for the new one.

This lightening, from things, from negative interactions, from bad habits, will give you a feeling of extreme lightness: you may come back with possessive energies that you did not even expect to have.

Year 9 is a powerful passage and, to be sure

you are in the right direction, it is advisable to wait for the second part of the year to give life to the projects you had in the drawer.

In fact, it is likely that the first six months will be dedicated to melting the knots still on the path of your personal change. Let the results come out on their own.

Keywords for Year 9: Close, Listen, Learn.

25
HOW TO USE NUMEROLOGY

Numerology is the study of numbers and their meaning.

It is a discipline based on the concept that the name you have received from your parents, the day, month, and year of your birth contains all the information that is closely related to you and, if thoroughly studied, can reveal important aspects of your Your personality and your life.

Numerology is an ancient tradition, as we have already explained in the introduction, and has involved many scholars, being used thousands of years ago in China, Greece, Rome and Egypt, even long before Pythagoras, considered Father of numerology.

In numerological analysis, the numeric value of the letters that make up your name and surname and the numbers of your date of birth are added in various ways, thus creating a real personal profile. The Numerologist has the task of interpreting these figures and suggesting any reflections and insights on important life decisions.

Why Request a Numerical Chart?

The main reason might be to be aware of ourselves, of our potentialities.

However, we may also need to go further and make it easier for us to accept ourselves, for how we are and to make some changes based on the information we receive.

Your Numerical Chart contains a general

view of your natural talents, the purpose of your life, your motivations, how others see you, your actions and reactions, any deficiencies and what your basic character tells you.

Numerology allows you to increase your awareness, allows you to take a more objective view of your personality and can help you understand the general path of the path you chose.

As you enter the description of your numbers, you will begin to open to the understanding they themselves contain.

Accepting yourself is the first conscious action to accomplish and making it creates serenity and stability. You will discover, in addition to your talents, the desires and the lessons to learn in life.

Additionally, your Numerical Card may also indicate the years and months in which, presumably, there may be major changes in your existence, giving you the information you need to decide on it.

There are several applications of Numerology. You can edit the name, name, surname, surname and date of birth and get the Numerical Table for each of these sectors:

- Couple Affinity - Identify the key points to improve interaction between partners

- Naming Company - The Importance of Company Name and Trademark, Decrease Its Potential

- Baby Name - Analyze the name and date of the baby to favor its growth in harmony and awareness

- Numerological Chart - Complete examination of the person, includes the psychological, relational and professional aspects

- Free Analysis - Creating a specific question,

formulated for a decision to take or to find a solution to a problem to be solved.

These are, in summary, the most frequent numerical processing. As you can see, it is possible to distance ourselves to this request because, the numbers that represent us, completely cover our Personal Universe and allow us to examine it even in separate sections.

26
FINAL THOUGHT

Numerology to grow

Using the numbers to better understand your life is almost like exploring subterranean, complex and extensively, illuminating them with a powerful bundle of direct light.

We do not always find the best direction right away and that is why, with patience and tenacity, we must learn to know more deeply.

Our numbers can help us in this journey.

This little book intends to bring the reader closer to this fascinating discipline and lead him to find himself again, through his own numerical traits.

The Numerological Card represents our personal Mandala, just like the chart of our astrological Christmas theme.

Find the time to take care of yourself, your soul's needs, and listen to the needs of your heart.

For me, what I wish you, is that the next twelve months are, and represent, the true turning point, what you have been waiting for a long time.

I wish you, the New Year, for you the wonderful year in which you will be able to fulfill the most important wishes.

Along with this wish, I leave you with the invitation to firmly believe in your dreams. Be yourself the strength capable of achieving them!

Do not give up on your maximum

expression, your personal accomplishment. You are born with special talents and you have the duty (besides the right) to manifest them, to express them, to enrich your life and your neighbor.

Good life!

Vitiana Paola Montana

Counselor & Kabalistic Coaching©

www.vitianapaolamontana.it

Made in the USA
Columbia, SC
14 February 2018